Snowflakes to Glaciers, a Wild Alaska Story

Written by Taylor Hoku Hayden

Illustrated by Molly Trainor

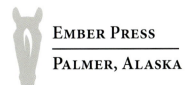

EMBER PRESS
PALMER, ALASKA

Text © 2019 Taylor Hoku Hayden
Illustrations © 2019 Molly Trainor

All rights reserved. No part of this book may be reproduced or transmitted in any form or by any means, electronic or mechanical, including photocopying, recording, or by any information storage and retrieval system, without written consent of the publisher.

Library of Congress Control Number: 2018963511
ISBN: 978-0-9986883-6-7

Book design: Nanette Stevenson
Cover design: Molly Trainor and Nanette Stevenson

Printed in Korea by Four Colour Print Group
Production Date: 11.6.18
Plant & Location: Printed by We SP Corp., Seoul, Korea
Job / Batch #78788-0/WeSP032217

Distributed by Ember Press and the Kenai Mountains–Turnagain Arm National Heritage Area

The Kenai Mountains–Turnagain Arm (KMTA) National Heritage Area
is one of the forty-nine Heritage Areas across the nation, and Alaska's first.
The KMTA National Heritage Area was established in 2009 through an act of Congress
to recognize, preserve, and interpret the historic resources and cultural landscapes of
the Kenai Mountains–Turnagain Arm transportation corridor.
kmtacorridor.org

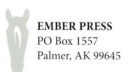

EMBER PRESS
PO Box 1557
Palmer, AK 99645

EmberPressBooks.com

To my mom — T H H

To my beautiful family, who nurtured an environment of total chaos and reckless disregard for personal space. Quyanna! — M T

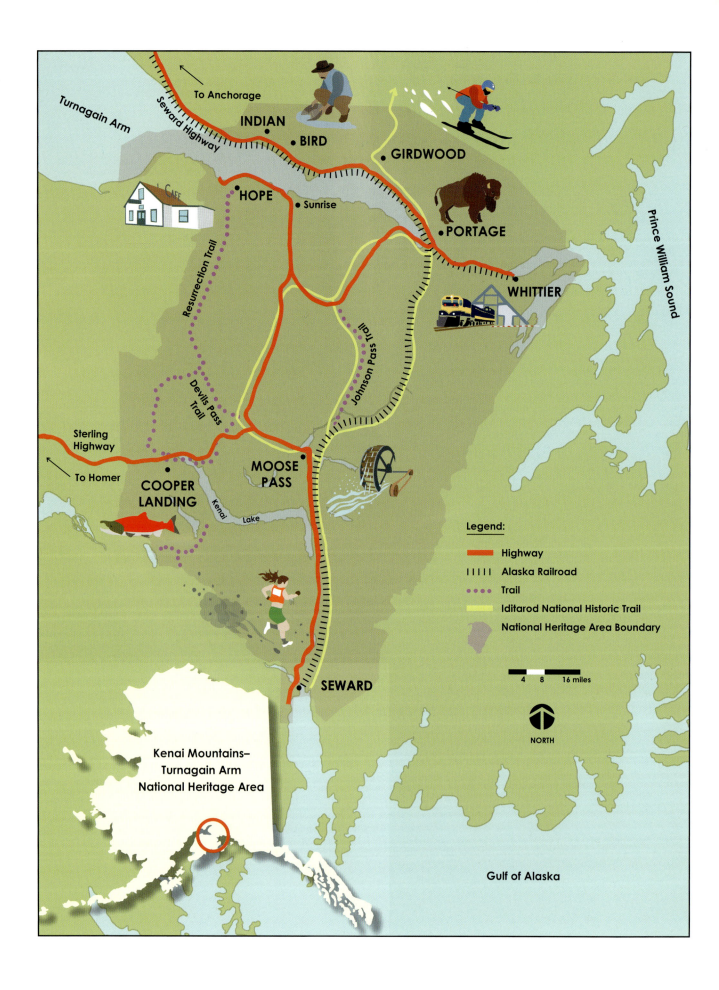

Discover the Story

✳ The Kenai Mountains–Turnagain Arm (KMTA) National Heritage Area is one of forty-nine across the United States, and Alaska's first. National Heritage Areas are places that tell the stories of our nation's history.

✳ Water helped shape this land. For thousands of years, glaciers carved deep valleys, leaving behind lakes, rivers, and streams. Glaciers form when more snow falls than melts season after season. As heavy snow piles up, it turns to ice. Today the earth is warmer, and most glaciers in Alaska are melting.

✳ Early people of the area often used water as a means of transportation. In the summer they traveled in boats made of animal skins. In winter they used frozen rivers and lakes to walk to neighboring villages. They fished and hunted and lived along fresh water and the ocean.

✳ Explorers came here by ship from other lands. Turnagain Arm was named because Captain James Cook had to "turn again" when he discovered this waterway was an inlet, not a river leading to the Northwest Passage.

✳ Russians also came to Alaska by boat. They built a ship, the *Phoenix*, in the harbor of Resurrection Bay near today's town of Seward.

✳ In the late 1800s, gold miners worked in creeks and used water to wash away rocks and silt to find gold. Water has also been used to generate electricity, like the waterwheel at Moose Pass.

✳ Snow falls. Glaciers calve. Rivers flow. Mist rises. Smoke swirls. Rain falls again. The cycle of water is the cycle of life. Follow along as water, in its many forms, makes a journey through the Kenai Mountains–Turnagain Arm National Heritage Area.

As the ripples settle, Water drifts away from Glacier.

"Hello, Iceberg," says Beaver.

"I'm not Iceberg," says Water. "I'm Glacier."

"You were once only Glacier," says Beaver. "But now you are also Iceberg."

"I am?" asks Water.

"You are." And with a slap of the tail, Beaver swims off.

Morning warms into day. Black Bear leads her cubs along Lake's shore.

"Hello, Lake," says Black Bear.

"I'm not Lake," says Water. "I'm Iceberg."

"You were once only Iceberg," says Black Bear. "But now you are also Lake."

"So I am," says Water. "I am Lake, melted from Iceberg, born of the great, ancient Glacier."

Water laps along the wooded shore. Darkened by thunderheads, the air turns sticky and fitful. Lightning splits the sky, igniting the brush. As the fire burns, water vapor billows upward, swirling with ash and soot.

Dall Sheep scales the valley walls, charging ahead of the fire.

"Hello, Smoke," says Dall Sheep.

"I'm not Smoke," says Water. "I'm Lake."

"You were once only Lake," says Dall Sheep. "But now you are also Smoke."

"I am Smoke," says Water, "once from Lake, melted from Iceberg, born of the great, ancient Glacier."

As ash and soot fall away, Water swells and gathers, forming tiny droplets.
"Hello, Rain," says Eagle.
"I'm not Rain," says Water. "I'm Smoke."
"You were once only Smoke," says Eagle. "But now you are also Rain."

"I am Rain, gathered from Smoke, once from Lake, melted from Iceberg, born of the great, ancient Glacier," says Water. In big drops, Water hurtles down, leaving traces of a misty rainbow.

Water rolls toward a bed of small pebbles where Silver Salmon spawns.
"Hello, River," says Silver Salmon.
"Hello, Salmon," says Water, which is now also River.

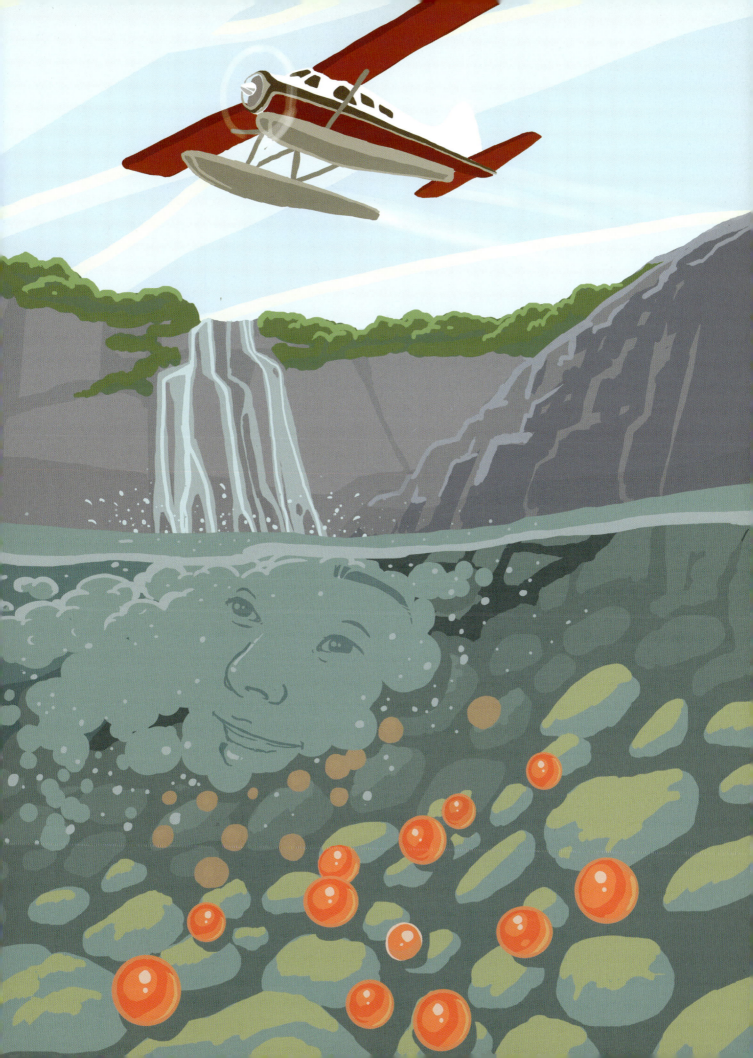

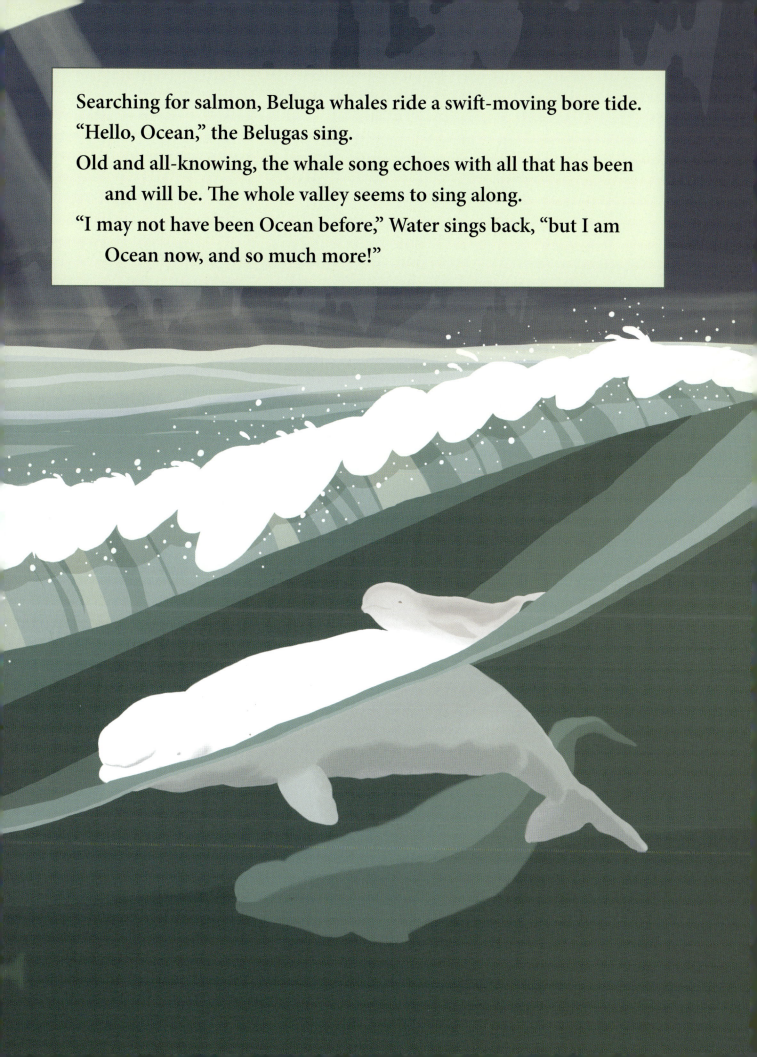

Searching for salmon, Beluga whales ride a swift-moving bore tide.
"Hello, Ocean," the Belugas sing.
Old and all-knowing, the whale song echoes with all that has been and will be. The whole valley seems to sing along.
"I may not have been Ocean before," Water sings back, "but I am Ocean now, and so much more!"

"I am Ocean, River, Rain, Smoke, Lake, Iceberg, born of the great, ancient Glacier," says Water.
Water rises from Ocean to where cold Wind nips the air.
"Hello, Cloud," says Wind.
"I have become so much already," says Water, "and now I am also Cloud."
Dancing and swirling, Wind whispers, "Yes, you are. And there's more."

All grows quiet. Slowly, weightlessly, Water drifts from the sky. Moose raises her head. A fluffy flake lands on her warm nose.
"Hello, Snow," Moose says.
Nestling into a soft bed of white, Water makes no reply.

Year after year, snow piles upon snow. Where the journey began, it begins again.
"Hello, Water," says Raven.

Cycle of Water

Condensation | Precipitation | Evaporation

DID YOU KNOW?

❄ Alaska has more than 3 million lakes, over 12,000 rivers, thousands of streams and creeks, and about 100,000 glaciers.

❄ Alaska is home to more than 40 percent of our nation's surface water.

❄ Three-fourths of all freshwater in Alaska is stored as glacial ice.

❄ Glacial ice covers nearly 5 percent of the state.